Higher Plans

FINANCIAL TRACKING WORKBOOK

A God Idea Developed for Kingdom Believers to
Effectively Track, Experience, and Maintain Financial Wealth

Debt Freedom   Surplus Funds   Higher Investments

Verbateen Wilson

WESTBOW®
PRESS
A DIVISION OF THOMAS NELSON
& ZONDERVAN

WestBow Press books may be ordered through booksellers or by contacting:

WestBow Press
A Division of Thomas Nelson & Zondervan
1663 Liberty Drive
Bloomington, IN 47403
www.westbowpress.com
1 (866) 928-1240

ISBN: 978-1-4908-8410-3 (sc)
ISBN: 978-1-4908-8411-0 (e)

Print information available on the last page.

WestBow Press rev. date: 09/04/2015

Name: _____

Date: _____

Dedication

This workbook is for my daughter, Verbatina, and all God's believers around the world. Be creative and profitable.

Acknowledgments

Thank you, God, for giving a God idea; thank you, Jesus, for saving me and allowing me to experience kingdom ideas; thank you, Holy Spirit, for directing me in the completion of this *Higher Plans* idea.

Contents

Introduction

Most of us have suffered and are still suffering from financial stress, which can ultimately destroy us if we don't make and maintain eye contact with God to see our way out. God's plan for your life is still in effect until further notice from Him. The enemy displays many materialistic things that cause us to become weakened in our righteous lifestyle. We forget to live to entertain God and instead slip into the trap of entertaining the world and allowing the world to entertain the children of God. The world has so much to offer, but we cannot forget that God owns it all and that He is the ultimate shifter; He will shift from the ungodly hands to the righteous hands, and the righteous will experience Him shifting in every season.

As a believer, you cannot afford to live in the wilderness (a worldly lifestyle of disobedience) anymore. We, the believers, live in this world, but we don't think as the world does. Our minds have been voted into God's kingdom, which is now Jesus Christ's and not our own or anyone else's. His kingdom gives us a new way of living life on Earth; we must live up to His standards and His commands to avoid the weakness of financial hardship in perilous times. Personal financial deficit can cause relationships to become troubled and health to deteriorate; the one can and will affect the other. The enemy's goals are to kill, steal, and destroy, but we must remember Christ and that He came to give us life-the very thing the enemy is trying to conquer. For this reason, it is very important that you disconnect yourself from debts owed and owe no one anymore. When doing this, you must allow the Holy Spirit to guide your finances. I beg that you do not come against the leading of the Holy Spirit, but fully surrender, as this is one of the ways to accomplish the plans God has already set for you. Remember, God has higher plans for His chosen; by remaining faithful His promises to you will come to pass. Please note that in order to hear the voice of God concerning your finances, you must surrender yourself and become a surrendered vessel, holy to the Lord.

When referring to the Holy Bible, I am reminded of how God owned Elijah's vessel and Enoch's vessel, just to name a few. If you become a willing surrendered vessel, He will perform his ways in you and through you more than you could ever imagine. Some of us are stiff, because of selfish ways that are not of God. Yes, even the believers need to be delivered from ourselves before it's too late. The world is in a danger zone, and at any moment, a great famine can arrive. As children of God, we must remember that God will send relief to His own. He will allow us to live in the land and be fed, and He will care for us. The abundance of wealth must reign in our daily lives so that we have additional surplus funds to care for orphans and widows. Debts are lingering in many believers' households and churches, a stronghold that must end immediately through the loosening of our debts so that freedom can be our release. The world system is in debt, and the world will always be in debt; trillions of dollars are owed between countries and between people. My brothers and sisters it is important that we see ourselves release from financial stronghold. When the great and the small financial famines' winds blow, you must know that you are anchored in God's higher plans for your life. Yes, you can be debt free; just keep your spiritual eyes on God. Yes, you can have extras; just keep your spiritual eyes on God. Yes, you can invest in having your own business and much more; just keep your spiritual eyes on God, fasten your spiritual ears to His mouth, and listen to His direction every step of the way.

Now is the time to allow God's higher plans to immediately turn around your finances. Now is the time to believe more, speak word of life over your finances, and to apply what you believe so that God's higher plan will manifest throughout the seasons. The drought is over and the pain from lacking money is over, because you believe it's over. Now God will perform miracles in your life and send favor after favor your way. God's abundance belongs to the body of Christ. You must take financial action to experience His abundance. There are many believers who have never experienced debt and those who got out of debt. I pray that we will seek God through prayer and fasting on behalf of our brothers and sisters who are in debt, that they will soon come out of debt so that they can experience God's abundance here on Earth.

Higher Financial Plans

One day while in Central Park during lunch, I sought the Lord concerning my lack of finances. Like most of you, I paid my full tithes, not merely tips, and gave offerings, as required for a believer of God, but I was still trapped in debt for many years. Money holes were in my pockets, and most of the time I could not account for the money I misused. The Lord instructed me with a plan, not just for myself but also for all who experience what I experienced. Remember, this world's financial enemy doesn't want you to prosper in abundance as a child of God. Due to that fact, my mind was made up, and I was desperately ready to trust God all the way concerning my finances. I no longer wanted to participate in unstable thinking and decided instead to think like Christ. The instructions and power of God's Word taught me how to take command of things that concern me by speaking commanding words and seeing them manifest. Because I believe the Lord, I spoke His Word, and I applied what I believed; I became debt-free from a debt of $13,000.00 within eleven months. During that time, and still today, the Holy Spirit has taught me how to keep track of every coin and dollar that is placed in my hand and how to avoid craving material things that are not of value. Though this financial tracking workbook may seem like it's just another workbook to try, don't be deceived; trust in the Lord and live by His Word, and favor and miracles will manifest for believers. As you continue to track your finances, God will approve your diligence and faithfulness. The days of financial instability are over.

Will I Benefit from the Higher Plans Workbook?

The Higher Plans workbook is for believers of all ages. You are never too young or too old to learn about God's finances the holy way. The Holy Spirit wants to guide us higher; are you ready? Please don't miss out on what should belong to you or become so lacking in knowledge that you miss God and have to seek the world for financial aid. I believe this workbook will address areas that many Kingdom believers, some like me, have been waiting for. I pray that this workbook will assist you with coming out of debt and keep you out of debt, and that it will take you higher in the financial plans God has already set for you.

Higher Plans' Foundational Scripture

"For I know the plans I have for you," declares the Lord, "plans to prosper you and not to harm you, plans to give you hope and a future." (Jeremiah 29:11)(NIV)

Reference scriptures to research, study and apply:

1. Malachi 3:8-11

2. Deuteronomy 28

3. Hebrews 11:1

4. Romans 12:1-2

5. Psalm 115:14

6. Matthew 6:33

7. Habakkuk 2:2-3

8. Proverbs 3

9. Psalm 23

10. Proverbs 16:3

11. Isaiah 25:1

12. 1 Peter 1:15-16

13. 2 Peter 1:10-11

14. Numbers 23:19

15. Exodus 3:8-9

16. Psalm 1

17. Psalm 118:17

18. Psalm 37

19. Ephesians 4:30

20. Ecclesiastes 3:10

The Plans

Once I got out of debt, I had very little money remaining in my bank account. I am very blessed to experience that God truly keeps His promises. I don't know about you, but in the past, I had problems saving money in my bank account. It seems that once I got to a certain amount in my account, it decreased. Unexpected bills would come, and this kept me in debt with a low bank balance. The Spirit of truth opened my eyes for me to see a repeated pattern taking place. I realized that the words I spoke played a major part in being in debt and lacking sufficient funds.

My way of thinking and living changed for the good. After almost fifteen years of being in debt, it finally happened: He got me out of debt. I am still amazed by His performance in my life. Now with great excitement, seeing my surplus-fund account continue to increase is proof to me that I can have as much as I believe I can have and much more. Currently, I am working on my Higher Investment plans; I expect to accomplish and enjoy many Higher Investment plans. As Kingdom believers, we must remain faithful to God in order to receive His financial direction for life. Please allow the leading of the Holy Spirit to govern your wealth.

Below are three plans you can choose from to begin the process to achieve what God already set for you. Maybe you are not in debt but need to secure extra money or maybe you are looking to go into business. Whatever you choose, I am asking you to remain faithful and complete the plan or plans.

Debt Freedom: Freedom from debt is vital to the kingdom's lifestyle. God will provide you with a way out, and the ability to overcome financial obstacles such as lack and hindrances that come from your decisions, or the decisions you accept from the enemy. Obedience to the instruction of the Holy Spirit will bring you into a debt- freedom lifestyle.

Surplus Fund: Establishing a surplus fund for your household is very important. Future uncertainties such as global famine or personal famines may arrive suddenly. Keeping your financial books in God's order is critical. By using this workbook, the Holy Spirit may lead you into establishing more than one surplus fund account. Check first with the Holy Spirit when making your financial decisions. Having more than enough is a blessed position to be in and an opportunity to be a blessing to others.

Higher Investments: Perhaps you are already debt-free and have surpluses set aside and are now ready to accomplish short and long-term plans. You will begin to comprehend higher and creative levels of thinking and the ability to obtain what God already set for you. Many Kingdom believers are looking to start their own business or purchase a home. The Higher Investment Plan is reachable for those who desire to reach higher.

Debt Freedom (Example)

My spirit will not become hindered due to credit card debt anymore. My bank account will not lack anymore. I am blessed, and I speak words of peace and power over my life daily. I am a daughter of the Most High God, and I faithfully without doubts pay my full tithes on time and give my full offering of investing seeds. I could see and smell the harvest of plenty, and I can say today that I have begun to experience tasting the harvest. My prayer is to keep seeing, smelling, and tasting in-season and out-of-season harvests. When I became clear from debts, I grew in wisdom and began to understand and experience what God wanted me to experience in Him all along: freedom from financial stronghold. The days of personally making unsure and worldly decisions are over; I surrendered all decision-making to the Holy Spirit, before I make a messy move. In eleven months, I became free from $13,000 of debt. The Holy Spirit informed me when to go shopping, how much to spend, and how to calculate my paychecks. I must admit that I was a little uneasy at first when the Holy Spirit told me to pay out my entire paychecks toward my tithes, offerings, common budget bills (food, light bill, etc.), and credit card debt, and not save anything. My savings overall had a total of approximately $100 or less.

Once I got accustomed to the way I spent money and paid bills, God's favor and miracles began to manifest in my life regularly. The Lord allowed my enemy to get a job during a recession, so I could get paid the money owed to me. The money I received was put toward paying down my debts. That is God's favor. I continue to believe God and experience the harvest He wants me to have. I always speak the living Word over my paychecks and additional income. Below is an example of my debt-free worksheet. I chose to begin my calculation by working my way from the bottom of the worksheet to the top as a reminder to me that I am coming out of debt's pits to come up higher in God's kingdom financial plans. Again, you may choose to process standard accounting calculation from top to bottom; it will also give you the same results: victory.

▨ Higher Plans Tracking (worksheet)

Completed Date: <u>August 29, 2009</u>

	Date and Record	Progress	Apply the Word
4	Oct. 16th Paid *(I received an additional "favor" check in the mail)*	$1,200.00	The rich rule over the poor, and the borrower becomes the lender's slave. *(Proverbs 22:7)*
3	Balance Due	($12,650.00)	My people are destroyed for lack of knowledge. *(Hosea. 4:6)*
2	Aug. 28th Paid	$350.00	…and thou shall lend unto many nations, but you will not borrow. *(Deuteronomy 15:6)*
1	Starting Balance Due	($13,000.00)	Forgive me of debt, as I forgive my debtors. *(paraphrase)* *(Matt 6:12)*

Higher Plan Name: <u>Debt Freedom</u>   **Target Date:** <u>Aug 2009</u>

Description: <u>Total credit card debts $13,000.00.</u>

Surplus Fund (Example)

She is twenty years old (we will call her Miss Spender). Miss Spender started the Higher Plans in August of 2009. She doesn't have credit card or loan debts. Freedom from debt is an awesome place to be, especially when you are very young. However, she is having difficulty in maintaining good stewardship over the finances God released to her. Though she pays her full tithes and gives her offering, she saves very little money in her account. Her shopping addiction held her back from reaching the kingdom's financial plan. After meeting with her one on one at first, she was not serious about using the workbook, until I informed her of the benefit of having all that God wants her to have and that the workbook is just an assisting guide. She did not mind increasing in the abundance of God, neither did she have any problem using the workbook to track her finances. Her struggle was that she would need to fully surrender to the Holy Spirit, draw closer to God through His Word, and speak and apply what she believed. As a starter, I helped her by praying with her and showing her the influx of her income and expense account. She has no liabilities, and little by little she is moving in the correct financial path. She was used to saving approximately $160 to $200 a month. Once she took heed to using the workbook, she saved approximately $800 within her first month. Soon she was locked into not only believing that the Word of God works, but she also believed she could become financially wealthy within the Kingdom of God. If she continues, she will reach and complete her first surplus fund plan and many more.

Below is an example of her tracking:

📈 Thirty-One Days' Shopping Log (worksheet)

Today's date	Description	Amount
8/1/09	Withdrawal from checking	40.00
8/1/09	Deodorant (debit card)	3.49
8/1/09	Movie (debit card)	14.00
8/1/09	Fast food –burger and fries (debit card)	8.99
8/2/09	Fast food- chicken (debit card)	10.32

📈 Calculate Income and Expenses (worksheet)

Aug 20, 2009 (Pay Check)		Sept 3, 2009 (Pay Check)	
Tithes & offering:	$164.40	Tithes & Offering:	$174.00
Surplus Fund:	**$323.60**	Surplus Fund:	**$500.00**
Food bill:	$70.00	Food bill:	$70.00
Rent:	$120.00	Rent:	$120.00
Cable:	$125.00	Me-money:	$80.00
Cell phone:	$91.00	Total:	**$944.00**
Me- money:	$50.00		
Total:	**$944.00**		

Surplus Fund (Example) continued...

⊠ **Higher Plans Tracking (worksheet)**

Completed Date: _____

	▼ Date and Record	▼ Progress	▼ Apply the Word
1	Current amount in Savings Account	2,000.00	The Lord is my Shepherd I shall not want. *(Psalm 23:1)*
2	Aug 20, 2009 deposited into Savings Account	**323.60**	Cast your bread upon the waters... *(Ecclesiastes 11:1)*
3	**Subtotal**	2,323.60	Thank you Lord.
4	Sept 3, 2009 deposited Savings Account	**500.00**	I will spend less and save more.

▲ ▲ ▲

Higher Plan Name: Surplus Fund #1   **Target Date:** Oct. 30, 2010
Description: To accumulate $10,000.00 for Surplus Fund #1.

Higher Investments (Example)

I am grateful to be working and receiving paychecks. Most financial experts says if you want to live financially comfortable, you need to either work more than one job or own a striving business. I can't picture myself working several jobs to live financially comfortable or to make ends meet. I cried out to the Lord; I needed a plan from God that would not burden my soul as the world claims. I believe God; I trust God for His peace, directions and resources in my life. After coming out of debt, my heart was set on owning my own business. By faith, I began to put money aside; little by little my investment account increased while I continued to save in my surplus account.

Staring your own business is rewarding and exciting. During the time I got out of debt, as promised, my job was to share with Kingdom believers how it was done. Creating this workbook was mandatory so that others could experience my passion for being debt- free, and my desire for others to become the same. I believe that this is one of many plans God has planted within me to carry-out. God is truly working on behalf of His children to get us our expected harvest of increases. He is reviving believers and extending their financial territory. As I continue to activate financial authority, I expect more favors and miracles to manifest.

Below is an example of how I creatively chose to use the tracking system to track my investment plan transactions. Use Higher Plans tracking system to start and maintain all your business needs.

⌧ Higher Plans Tracking (worksheet)

Completed Date: _____

▼ Date and Record	▼ Progress	▼ Apply the Word
Mar. 27, 2010 – deposit in investment acct.	$500.00	Enlarge my border… *(1 Chr 4:10)*
SUBTOTAL	**$550.00**	Thank you Lord.
Feb. 15, 2010 – deposit in investment acct.	$400.00	Complete a business plan by June 2010.
Dec. 1, 2009 -first deposit for business	$150.00	For the Lord your God is bringing you into a good land… *(Deut. 8:7)*

▲   ▲   ▲

Higher Plan Name: Higher Investment   **Target Date:** Jan. 1, 2011
Description: Invest in starting first business to extend my territory.

Work the Plans Detail

The Higher Plans system is a unique kingdom economic accounting system that is created for Kingdom believers. Faithfully use the accounting sheets to calculate and track all income funds and expenses. Your success depends on your obedience to the voice of the Holy Spirit. Taking this financial pathway, you will experience the increases in your assets and income and the decreases in your liabilities and expenses. Higher Plans is a powerful tracking system that will help you develop and maintain financial growth. Below are the names and details of each worksheet.

Tithes & Offerings Tracking Worksheet: This is my interpretation and experience of tithes and offerings. My tithes are considered "kingdom taxes," which cover my lifeline of health, relationships and finances. My offerings are considered "kingdom investment seeds" that bring about favor and miracles and a harvest in all seasons. Please refer to the Holy Bible's scriptures pertaining to tithing and offering. Every believer needs to be married to this principle. If you are not, trust God and begin. The Tithes & Offering indicator is the blueprint of everything you will experience while using this workbook; it is specially designed as a reminder to yourself that you are a participator in God's kingdom.

Below is an example of how to track your tithes and offerings. You can choose to enter the dollar amount or enter Yes for paid or No for not paid. This is a great way for you to see where you stand and how you can improve. This reflects one of the reasons why we are not financially successful. If you don't have tithes and offerings (meaning no income at all) you should seek the Lord in prayer for an income breakthrough. If you receive income, your tracking sheets should be complete with the dollar amount.

⊞ Tithes and Offerings Worksheet

	Date	Amount
Tithe	3/7/10	$300.23
Offering	3/7/10	$25.00
Tithe	3/14/10	No
Offering	3/14/10	$125.00

Three Months' Total Report Worksheet: This is an important overall view of where you currently stand financially. Before you begin, you must first take time to list total kingdom assets and liabilities or expenses to the report sheet. Whether you are in debt or not, it is good to review the big picture before beginning Higher Plan. Use this report to list totals of your entire assets (such as checking account, 401K, etc.) and enter the expense total (enter the total credit cards and other loans debt amounts). Others expenses such as cable bills, food bills, etc. must be entered in an estimated three- month total. Every three months, you will prepare a new report by calculating the change in your finances, and reviewing your progress of increase or decrease to your kingdom assets or liabilities/expenses.

⊠ Three Months' Total Report Worksheet:

Kingdom Assets	Amount	Liabilities/Expenses	Amount
1. Diamond ring	$950.00 (value)	1. Credit Cards (total amount)	$12,000.00
2. Savings Account	$1,500.00	2. Monthly cable bill (3 month estimate)	$475.00

Thirty-one Days' Shopping Log Worksheet: The enemy's job is to keep you broke! The world's system is designed to keep you in poverty. This needed shopping log simply provides you with an opportunity to review how much you are spending on things that are not a part of your common kingdom budget. (Common kingdom budget list contains groceries, light bill, gas bill, etc.). Your monthly challenge will be to record your daily spending during the thirty-one days and the next thirty-one days. Going forward, you will seek to reduce your spending to a minimum until you become a wise, confident shopper.

Optional: Use a color marker to highlight items that you need to cut out (reduce your spending habits) and you will clearly see why your kingdom financial wealth is stagnating. Also, to use this sheet wisely, you should retain all purchase receipts and update this sheet once a week or when you update other sheets in this workbook.

⊠ Thirty-One Days' Shopping Log Worksheet:

Today's date	Description	Amount
3/4/10	Large mocha latte	5.79
3/5/10	Lunch – burger, fries & shake	8.87
3/5/10	Toothpaste	3.49

Thirty-One Days Total Amount:	$18.15
Total amount of wise spending in Thirty-one Days:	$3.49
Total amount of money squandered in Thirty-one Days:	$14.76

Calculate Income & Expenses Worksheet is used to calculate all income such as payroll checks, rebates, refunds, royalties, unexpected checks in the mail, money found in the streets, favor money, etc., and all expenses such as the light bill, food bill, gas bill, credit card, loans, rent, etc. The purpose of using the calculating sheet is to determine the amount of money you will enter on your Higher Plans Tracking Worksheet. It is critical that you use both the calculating sheet along with the Higher Plan Tracking Worksheet.

Higher Plans Tracking Worksheet: This specially designed worksheet gives you the option to enter and calculate from the top to the bottom like normal accounting systems, or you have the option to enter and calculate from the bottom of the worksheet to the top. Whichever way is performed, the outcome will be the same. Use additional worksheets if needed until you have completed the plan. Remember to first use the calculating sheet, which will help you decide what amount to enter on the plan (Debt Freedom, Surplus Fund, or Higher Plans Investment) you selected.

Higher Plans Tracking Worksheet continued:

Date and Record	Progress	Apply the Word

1. You can decide to number your transaction top to bottom, as is the normal accounting system custom or from bottom to the top as a creative challenge. The arrows are a transaction direction guide. Please remember that this is kingdom processing, not the norm you are accustomed to.

2. **Date and Record:** Keep track of all transactions by entering deposit dates, debt payoff dates, and investment plan record-keeping.

3. **Progress:** Record all money transactions. To maintain accurate accounting, remember to enter subtotal dollar amount.

4. **Apply the Word:** To apply the Word of God, you must be in position to receive instructions. By faith, study, speak, command, and apply the Word of God which is the power seed to your divine harvest. The Holy Spirit will encourage you to go higher in the plans God already set for you. Believe God for debt freedom, more favors, and financial miracles. Remember, to experience results and base it on the Word of God, it is critical that you process this workbook in its entirety.

5. Select and enter the name of the plan (Debt Freedom, Surplus Fund, or Higher Plan Investment plans).

6. Enter a realistic target date, the one the Holy Spirit revealed to you.

7. Enter a description. The description will briefly remind you of your reason to fulfill the plan.

8. This worksheet can also be use to maintain bank transactions.

Write the Vision: Your financial higher kingdom plans are worth writing down, and to accomplish them, take as many notes from the Holy Spirit as possible. Go higher in the plans God already has established for you.

Vision Illustration: Illustrate your personal and business financial plans.

To assure that you achieve your Higher Plan, use all worksheets and organize and keep track of all incoming funds and expenses by placing them in individual folders to refer back to.

Remember that long-term prayer, fasting, meditating, studying and applying the Word of God is essential to the kingdom's lifestyle.

Tithes & Offerings Tracking

Bring the whole tithe into the storehouse... (Mal 3:10)

Tithes & Offerings Tracking

Malachi 3:8-11

	Date	Amount
Tithe		
Offering		
Tithe		
Offering		
Tithe		
Offering		
Tithe		
Offering		
Tithe		
Offering		
Tithe		
Offering		
Tithe		
Offering		
Tithe		
Offering		
Tithe		
Offering		
Tithe		
Offering		
Tithe		
Offering		
Tithe		
Offering		
Tithe		
Offering		

	Date	Amount
Tithe		
Offering		
Tithe		
Offering		
Tithe		
Offering		
Tithe		
Offering		
Tithe		
Offering		
Tithe		
Offering		
Tithe		
Offering		
Tithe		
Offering		
Tithe		
Offering		
Tithe		
Offering		
Tithe		
Offering		
Tithe		
Offering		
Tithe		
Offering		

Enter Additional Offering

date	amount	date	amount	date	amount	date	amount

Tithes & Offerings Tracking

Malachi 3:8-11

	Date	Amount
Tithe		
Offering		
Tithe		
Offering		
Tithe		
Offering		
Tithe		
Offering		
Tithe		
Offering		
Tithe		
Offering		
Tithe		
Offering		
Tithe		
Offering		
Tithe		
Offering		
Tithe		
Offering		
Tithe		
Offering		
Tithe		
Offering		

	Date	Amount
Tithe		
Offering		
Tithe		
Offering		
Tithe		
Offering		
Tithe		
Offering		
Tithe		
Offering		
Tithe		
Offering		
Tithe		
Offering		
Tithe		
Offering		
Tithe		
Offering		
Tithe		
Offering		
Tithe		
Offering		
Tithe		
Offering		

Enter Additional Offering

date	amount	date	amount	date	amount	date	amount

Tithes & Offerings Tracking

Malachi 3:8-11

	Date	Amount			Date	Amount
Tithe				**Tithe**		
Offering				Offering		
Tithe				**Tithe**		
Offering				Offering		
Tithe				**Tithe**		
Offering				Offering		
Tithe				**Tithe**		
Offering				Offering		
Tithe				**Tithe**		
Offering				Offering		
Tithe				**Tithe**		
Offering				Offering		
Tithe				**Tithe**		
Offering				Offering		
Tithe				**Tithe**		
Offering				Offering		
Tithe				**Tithe**		
Offering				Offering		
Tithe				**Tithe**		
Offering				Offering		
Tithe				**Tithe**		
Offering				Offering		
Tithe				**Tithe**		
Offering				Offering		

Enter Additional Offering

date	amount	date	amount	date	amount	date	amount

Tithes & Offerings Tracking

Malachi 3:8-11

	Date	Amount
Tithe		
Offering		
Tithe		
Offering		
Tithe		
Offering		
Tithe		
Offering		
Tithe		
Offering		
Tithe		
Offering		
Tithe		
Offering		
Tithe		
Offering		
Tithe		
Offering		
Tithe		
Offering		
Tithe		
Offering		
Tithe		
Offering		

	Date	Amount
Tithe		
Offering		
Tithe		
Offering		
Tithe		
Offering		
Tithe		
Offering		
Tithe		
Offering		
Tithe		
Offering		
Tithe		
Offering		
Tithe		
Offering		
Tithe		
Offering		
Tithe		
Offering		
Tithe		
Offering		
Tithe		
Offering		

Enter Additional Offering

date	amount	date	amount	date	amount	date	amount

Three Months' Total Report

Three Months' Total Report

Today's Date: _____

Kingdom Assets	Amount	Liabilities/Expenses	Amount
1. _____	_____	1. _____	_____
2. _____	_____	2. _____	_____
3. _____	_____	3. _____	_____
4. _____	_____	4. _____	_____
5. _____	_____	5. _____	_____
6. _____	_____	6. _____	_____
7. _____	_____	7. _____	_____
8. _____	_____	8. _____	_____
9. _____	_____	9. _____	_____
10. _____	_____	10. _____	_____
11. _____	_____	11. _____	_____
12. _____	_____	12. _____	_____
13. _____	_____	13. _____	_____
14. _____	_____	14. _____	_____
15. _____	_____	15. _____	_____
Total: _____		**Total:** _____	

Three Months' Total Report

Today's Date: _____

Kingdom Assets	Amount	Liabilities/Expenses	Amount
1. _____	_____	1. _____	_____
2. _____	_____	2. _____	_____
3. _____	_____	3. _____	_____
4. _____	_____	4. _____	_____
5. _____	_____	5. _____	_____
6. _____	_____	6. _____	_____
7. _____	_____	7. _____	_____
8. _____	_____	8. _____	_____
9. _____	_____	9. _____	_____
10. _____	_____	10. _____	_____
11. _____	_____	11. _____	_____
12. _____	_____	12. _____	_____
13. _____	_____	13. _____	_____
14. _____	_____	14. _____	_____
15. _____	_____	15. _____	_____
Total: _____		**Total:** _____	

Three Months' Total Report

Today's Date: _____

Kingdom Assets	Amount	Liabilities/Expenses	Amount
1. _____	_____	1. _____	_____
2. _____	_____	2. _____	_____
3. _____	_____	3. _____	_____
4. _____	_____	4. _____	_____
5. _____	_____	5. _____	_____
6. _____	_____	6. _____	_____
7. _____	_____	7. _____	_____
8. _____	_____	8. _____	_____
9. _____	_____	9. _____	_____
10. _____	_____	10. _____	_____
11. _____	_____	11. _____	_____
12. _____	_____	12. _____	_____
13. _____	_____	13. _____	_____
14. _____	_____	14. _____	_____
15. _____	_____	15. _____	_____
Total: _____		**Total:** _____	

Three Months' Total Report

Today's Date: _____

Kingdom Assets	Amount	Liabilities/Expenses	Amount
1. _____	_____	1. _____	_____
2. _____	_____	2. _____	_____
3. _____	_____	3. _____	_____
4. _____	_____	4. _____	_____
5. _____	_____	5. _____	_____
6. _____	_____	6. _____	_____
7. _____	_____	7. _____	_____
8. _____	_____	8. _____	_____
9. _____	_____	9. _____	_____
10. _____	_____	10. _____	_____
11. _____	_____	11. _____	_____
12. _____	_____	12. _____	_____
13. _____	_____	13. _____	_____
14. _____	_____	14. _____	_____
15. _____	_____	15. _____	_____
Total: _____		**Total:** _____	

Three Months' Total Report

Today's Date: _____

Kingdom Assets	Amount	Liabilities/Expenses	Amount
1. _____	_____	1. _____	_____
2. _____	_____	2. _____	_____
3. _____	_____	3. _____	_____
4. _____	_____	4. _____	_____
5. _____	_____	5. _____	_____
6. _____	_____	6. _____	_____
7. _____	_____	7. _____	_____
8. _____	_____	8. _____	_____
9. _____	_____	9. _____	_____
10. _____	_____	10. _____	_____
11. _____	_____	11. _____	_____
12. _____	_____	12. _____	_____
13. _____	_____	13. _____	_____
14. _____	_____	14. _____	_____
15. _____	_____	15. _____	_____
Total: _____		**Total:** _____	

Three Months' Total Report

Today's Date: _____

Kingdom Assets	Amount	Liabilities/Expenses	Amount
1. _____	_____	1. _____	_____
2. _____	_____	2. _____	_____
3. _____	_____	3. _____	_____
4. _____	_____	4. _____	_____
5. _____	_____	5. _____	_____
6. _____	_____	6. _____	_____
7. _____	_____	7. _____	_____
8. _____	_____	8. _____	_____
9. _____	_____	9. _____	_____
10. _____	_____	10. _____	_____
11. _____	_____	11. _____	_____
12. _____	_____	12. _____	_____
13. _____	_____	13. _____	_____
14. _____	_____	14. _____	_____
15. _____	_____	15. _____	_____
Total: _____		**Total:** _____	

Three Months' Total Report

Today's Date: _____

Kingdom Assets	Amount	Liabilities/Expenses	Amount
1. _____	_____	1. _____	_____
2. _____	_____	2. _____	_____
3. _____	_____	3. _____	_____
4. _____	_____	4. _____	_____
5. _____	_____	5. _____	_____
6. _____	_____	6. _____	_____
7. _____	_____	7. _____	_____
8. _____	_____	8. _____	_____
9. _____	_____	9. _____	_____
10. _____	_____	10. _____	_____
11. _____	_____	11. _____	_____
12. _____	_____	12. _____	_____
13. _____	_____	13. _____	_____
14. _____	_____	14. _____	_____
15. _____	_____	15. _____	_____
Total: _____		**Total:** _____	

Three Months' Total Report

Today's Date: _____

Kingdom Assets	Amount	Liabilities/Expenses	Amount
1. _____	_____	1. _____	_____
2. _____	_____	2. _____	_____
3. _____	_____	3. _____	_____
4. _____	_____	4. _____	_____
5. _____	_____	5. _____	_____
6. _____	_____	6. _____	_____
7. _____	_____	7. _____	_____
8. _____	_____	8. _____	_____
9. _____	_____	9. _____	_____
10. _____	_____	10. _____	_____
11. _____	_____	11. _____	_____
12. _____	_____	12. _____	_____
13. _____	_____	13. _____	_____
14. _____	_____	14. _____	_____
15. _____	_____	15. _____	_____
Total: _____		**Total:** _____	

Thirty-One Days' Shopping Log

And not many days later, the younger son gathered everything together and went on a journey into a distant country and there he squandered his estate with loose living. (**Luke 15:13**)

Thirty-One Days' Shopping Log

Today's date	Description	Amount

Thirty-one Days' Total Amount: _____

Total amount of wise spending in Thirty-one Days: _____

Total amount of money squandered in Thirty-one Days: _____

Thirty-One Days' Shopping Log

Today's date	Description	Amount

Thirty-one Days' Total Amount: _____

Total amount of wise spending in Thirty-one Days: _____

Total amount of money squandered in Thirty-one Days: _____

Thirty-One Days' Shopping Log

Today's date	Description	Amount

Thirty-one Days' Total Amount: _____

Total amount of wise spending in Thirty-one Days: _____

Total amount of money squandered in Thirty-one Days: _____

Thirty-One Days' Shopping Log

Today's date	Description	Amount

Thirty-one Days' Total Amount: _____

Total amount of wise spending in Thirty-one Days: _____

Total amount of money squandered in Thirty-one Days: _____

Thirty-One Days' Shopping Log

Today's date	Description	Amount

Thirty-one Days' Total Amount: _____

Total amount of wise spending in Thirty-one Days: _____

Total amount of money squandered in Thirty-one Days: _____

Thirty-One Days' Shopping Log

Today's date	Description	Amount

Thirty-one Days' Total Amount: _____

Total amount of wise spending in Thirty-one Days: _____

Total amount of money squandered in Thirty-one Days: _____

Thirty-One Days' Shopping Log

Today's date	Description	Amount

Thirty-one Days' Total Amount: _____

Total amount of wise spending in Thirty-one Days: _____

Total amount of money squandered in Thirty-one Days: _____

Thirty-One Days' Shopping Log

Today's date	Description	Amount

Thirty-one Days' Total Amount: _____

Total amount of wise spending in Thirty-one Days: _____

Total amount of money squandered in Thirty-one Days: _____

Thirty-One Days' Shopping Log

Today's date	Description	Amount

Thirty-one Days' Total Amount: _____

Total amount of wise spending in Thirty-one Days: _____

Total amount of money squandered in Thirty-one Days: _____

Thirty-One Days' Shopping Log

Today's date	Description	Amount

Thirty-one Days' Total Amount: _____

Total amount of wise spending in Thirty-one Days: _____

Total amount of money squandered in Thirty-one Days: _____

Thirty-One Days' Shopping Log

Today's date	Description	Amount

Thirty-one Days' Total Amount: _____

Total amount of wise spending in Thirty-one Days: _____

Total amount of money squandered in Thirty-one Days: _____

Thirty-One Days' Shopping Log

Today's date	Description	Amount

Thirty-one Days' Total Amount: _____

Total amount of wise spending in Thirty-one Days: _____

Total amount of money squandered in Thirty-one Days: _____

Thirty-One Days' Shopping Log

Today's date	Description	Amount

Thirty-one Days' Total Amount: _____

Total amount of wise spending in Thirty-one Days: _____

Total amount of money squandered in Thirty-one Days: _____

Thirty-One Days' Shopping Log

Today's date	Description	Amount

Thirty-one Days' Total Amount: _____

Total amount of wise spending in Thirty-one Days: _____

Total amount of money squandered in Thirty-one Days: _____

Thirty-One Days' Shopping Log

Today's date	Description	Amount

Thirty-one Days' Total Amount: _____

Total amount of wise spending in Thirty-one Days: _____

Total amount of money squandered in Thirty-one Days: _____

Thirty-One Days' Shopping Log

Today's date	Description	Amount

Thirty-one Days' Total Amount: _____

Total amount of wise spending in Thirty-one Days: _____

Total amount of money squandered in Thirty-one Days: _____

Thirty-One Days' Shopping Log

Today's date	Description	Amount

Thirty-one Days' Total Amount: _____

Total amount of wise spending in Thirty-one Days: _____

Total amount of money squandered in Thirty-one Days: _____

Thirty-One Days' Shopping Log

Today's date	Description	Amount

Thirty-one Days' Total Amount: _____

Total amount of wise spending in Thirty-one Days: _____

Total amount of money squandered in Thirty-one Days: _____

Calculate Income & Expenses

Calculate Income & Expenses

Calculate Income & Expenses

Calculate Income & Expenses

Calculate Income & Expenses

Calculate Income & Expenses

Calculate Income & Expenses

Calculate Income & Expenses

Calculate Income & Expenses

Calculate Income & Expenses

Calculate Income & Expenses

Calculate Income & Expenses

Higher Plans Tracking

Higher Plans Tracking

Date Completed: _____

▼	▼	▼
Date & Record	Progress	Apply the Word
▲	▲	▲

Higher Plan Name:_____ **Target Date:** _____

Description:_____

Higher Plans Tracking

Date Completed: _____

| ▼ | ▼ | ▼ |
Date & Record	Progress	Apply the Word

| ▲ | ▲ | ▲ |

Higher Plan Name:_____ **Target Date:** _____

Description:_____

Higher Plans Tracking

Date Completed: _____

▼   ▼   ▼

Date & Record	Progress	Apply the Word

▲   ▲   ▲

Higher Plan Name:_____ **Target Date:** _____

Description:_____

Higher Plans Tracking

Date Completed: _____

▼	▼	▼
Date & Record	Progress	Apply the Word
▲	▲	▲

Higher Plan Name:_____ **Target Date:** _____

Description:_____

Higher Plans Tracking

Date Completed: _____

▼   ▼   ▼

Date & Record	Progress	Apply the Word

▲   ▲   ▲

Higher Plan Name:_____ **Target Date:** _____

Description:_____

Higher Plans Tracking

Date Completed: _____

▼	▼	▼
Date & Record	Progress	Apply the Word
▲	▲	▲

Higher Plan Name:_____ **Target Date:** _____

Description:_____

Higher Plans Tracking

Date Completed: _____

▼   ▼   ▼

Date & Record	Progress	Apply the Word

▲   ▲   ▲

Higher Plan Name:_____ **Target Date:** _____

Description:_____

Higher Plans Tracking

Date Completed: _____

▼   ▼   ▼

Date & Record	Progress	Apply the Word

▲   ▲   ▲

Higher Plan Name:_____ **Target Date:** _____

Description:_____

Higher Plans Tracking

Date Completed: _____

▼	▼	▼
Date & Record	Progress	Apply the Word
▲	▲	▲

Higher Plan Name:_____ **Target Date:** _____

Description:_____

Higher Plans Tracking

Date Completed: _____

▼	▼	▼
Date & Record	Progress	Apply the Word
▲	▲	▲

Higher Plan Name:_____ **Target Date:** _____

Description:_____

Higher Plans Tracking

Date Completed: _____

▼ ▼ ▼

Date & Record	Progress	Apply the Word

▲ ▲ ▲

Higher Plan Name:_____ **Target Date:** _____

Description:_____

Higher Plans Tracking

Date Completed: _____

▼	▼	▼
Date & Record	Progress	Apply the Word
▲	▲	▲

Higher Plan Name:_____ **Target Date:** _____

Description:_____

Higher Plans Tracking

Date Completed: _____

▼   ▼   ▼

Date & Record	Progress	Apply the Word

▲   ▲   ▲

Higher Plan Name:_____ **Target Date:** _____

Description:_____

Higher Plans Tracking

Date Completed: _____

Date & Record	Progress	Apply the Word
▼	▼	▼
▲	▲	▲

Higher Plan Name:_____ **Target Date:** _____

Description:_____

Higher Plans Tracking

Date Completed: _____

▼   ▼   ▼

Date & Record	Progress	Apply the Word

▲   ▲   ▲

Higher Plan Name:_____ **Target Date:** _____

Description:_____

Higher Plans Tracking

Date Completed: _____

| | ▼ | ▼ | ▼ |
Date & Record	Progress	Apply the Word

▲   ▲   ▲

Higher Plan Name:_____ **Target Date:** _____

Description:_____

Higher Plans Tracking

Date Completed: _____

▼   ▼   ▼

Date & Record	Progress	Apply the Word

▲   ▲   ▲

Higher Plan Name: _____ **Target Date:** _____

Description: _____

Higher Plans Tracking

Date Completed: _____

| ▼ | ▼ | ▼ |
Date & Record	Progress	Apply the Word
▲	▲	▲

Higher Plan Name:_____ **Target Date:** _____

Description:_____

Higher Plans Tracking

Date Completed: _____

▼   ▼   ▼

Date & Record	Progress	Apply the Word

▲   ▲   ▲

Higher Plan Name:_____ **Target Date:** _____

Description:_____

Higher Plans Tracking

Date Completed: _____

▼   ▼   ▼

Date & Record	Progress	Apply the Word

▲   ▲   ▲

Higher Plan Name:_____ **Target Date:** _____

Description:_____

Higher Plans Tracking

Date Completed: _____

▼ ▼ ▼

Date & Record	Progress	Apply the Word

▲ ▲ ▲

Higher Plan Name:_____ **Target Date:** _____

Description:_____

Higher Plans Tracking

Date Completed: _____

▼	▼	▼
Date & Record	Progress	Apply the Word
▲	▲	▲

Higher Plan Name:_____ **Target Date:** _____

Description:_____

Higher Plans Tracking

Date Completed: _____

▼   ▼   ▼

Date & Record	Progress	Apply the Word

▲   ▲   ▲

Higher Plan Name: _____ **Target Date:** _____

Description: _____

Higher Plans Tracking

Date Completed: _____

▼　　　　　▼　　　　　　　▼

Date & Record	Progress	Apply the Word

▲　　　　　▲　　　　　　　▲

Higher Plan Name:_____ **Target Date:** _____

Description:_____

Higher Plans Tracking

Date Completed: _____

▼	▼	▼
Date & Record	Progress	Apply the Word
▲	▲	▲

Higher Plan Name:_____ **Target Date:** _____

Description:_____

Higher Plans Tracking

Date Completed: _____

▼   ▼   ▼

Date & Record	Progress	Apply the Word

▲   ▲   ▲

Higher Plan Name:_____ **Target Date:** _____

Description:_____

Higher Plans Tracking

Date Completed: _____

▼	▼	▼
Date & Record	Progress	Apply the Word
▲	▲	▲

Higher Plan Name:_____ **Target Date:** _____

Description:_____

Higher Plans Tracking

Date Completed: _____

▼　　　　　　　▼　　　　　　　　　▼

Date & Record	Progress	Apply the Word

▲　　　　　　　▲　　　　　　　　　▲

Higher Plan Name:_____ **Target Date:** _____

Description:_____

Higher Plans Tracking

Date Completed: _____

▼	▼	▼
Date & Record	Progress	Apply the Word
▲	▲	▲

Higher Plan Name:_____ **Target Date:** _____

Description:_____

Higher Plans Tracking

Date Completed: _____

▼   ▼   ▼

Date & Record	Progress	Apply the Word

▲   ▲   ▲

Higher Plan Name:_____ **Target Date:** _____

Description:_____

Higher Plans Tracking

Date Completed: _____

| ▼ | ▼ | ▼ |
Date & Record	Progress	Apply the Word

▲ ▲ ▲

Higher Plan Name:_____ **Target Date:** _____

Description:_____

Higher Plans Tracking

Date Completed: _____

▼ Date & Record	▼ Progress	▼ Apply the Word

▲   ▲   ▲

Higher Plan Name:_____ **Target Date:** _____

Description:_____

Higher Plans Tracking

Date Completed: _____

▼	▼	▼
Date & Record	Progress	Apply the Word
▲	▲	▲

Higher Plan Name:_____ **Target Date:** _____

Description:_____

Higher Plans Tracking

Date Completed: _____

▼	▼	▼
Date & Record	Progress	Apply the Word
▲	▲	▲

Higher Plan Name:_____ **Target Date:** _____

Description:_____

Higher Plans Tracking

Date Completed: _____

▼   ▼   ▼

Date & Record	Progress	Apply the Word

▲   ▲   ▲

Higher Plan Name:_____ **Target Date:** _____

Description:_____

Higher Plans Tracking

Date Completed: _____

▼ ▼ ▼

Date & Record	Progress	Apply the Word

▲ ▲ ▲

Higher Plan Name:_____ **Target Date:** _____

Description:_____

Write the Vision

For the vision is yet for the appointed time; it hastens toward the goal and it will not fail. Though it tarries, wait for it; for it will certainly come, it will not delay. (Habakkuk 2:3)

Write the Vision

Write the Vision

Write the Vision

Write the Vision

Write the Vision

Write the Vision

Write the Vision

Write the Vision

Write the Vision

Write the Vision

Write the Vision

Write the Vision

Write the Vision

Write the Vision

_____

_____

_____

_____

_____

_____

_____

_____

_____

_____

_____

_____

_____

_____

_____

_____

_____

_____

_____

_____

_____

_____

_____

_____

_____

_____

_____

_____

_____

_____

_____

_____

Write the Vision

_____
_____
_____
_____
_____
_____
_____
_____
_____
_____
_____
_____
_____
_____
_____
_____
_____
_____
_____
_____
_____
_____
_____
_____
_____
_____
_____
_____
_____
_____
_____
_____
_____

Write the Vision

Vision Illustration

Where there is no vision (no redemptive revelation of God), the people perish... (Proverb 29:18)

Vision Illustration

Vision Illustration

Vision Illustration

Vision Illustration

Vision Illustration

Vision Illustration

Vision Illustration

Vision Illustration

Vision Illustration

Vision Illustration

Vision Illustration

Vision Illustration

Vision Illustration

Vision Illustration

Vision Illustration

Vision Illustration